50 Brazilian Authentic Recipes

By: Kelly Johnson

Table of Contents

- Feijoada (Black Bean Stew)
- Pão de Queijo (Cheese Bread)
- Moqueca (Brazilian Fish Stew)
- Coxinha (Chicken Croquettes)
- Acarajé (Black-Eyed Pea Fritters)
- Vatapá (Seafood and Peanut Stew)
- Escondidinho de Carne Seca (Cassava and Dried Beef Casserole)
- Bobó de Camarão (Shrimp in Cassava Cream)
- Farofa (Toasted Cassava Flour)
- Arroz Carreteiro (Tropeiro's Rice)
- Tutu de Feijão (Mashed Beans with Flour)
- Carne de Sol (Sun-Dried Beef)
- Bolo de Rolo (Rolled Cake)
- Brigadeiro (Chocolate Fudge Balls)
- Quindim (Coconut Egg Custard)
- Beijinho (Coconut Truffle)
- Manjar Branco (Coconut Pudding)
- Pudim de Leite (Brazilian Flan)
- Canjica (Sweet Corn Pudding)
- Curau de Milho (Sweet Corn Custard)
- Cuscuz Paulista (Savory Cornmeal Cake)
- Empadão (Brazilian Pot Pie)
- Pastel (Fried Pastry with Filling)
- Bolinho de Bacalhau (Salt Cod Fritters)
- Caldo Verde (Green Soup)
- Sopa de Mandioquinha (Parsnip Soup)
- Baião de Dois (Rice and Beans with Cheese)
- Churrasco (Brazilian BBQ)
- Picanha (Grilled Top Sirloin)
- Frango com Quiabo (Chicken with Okra)
- Moela de Frango (Chicken Gizzards)
- Dobradinha (Tripe Stew)
- Arroz com Pequi (Rice with Pequi Fruit)
- Carne Louca (Shredded Beef Stew)
- Feijão Tropeiro (Pinto Beans with Sausage)

- Galinhada (Chicken and Rice)
- Espetinho de Coração (Grilled Chicken Hearts)
- Tapioca (Cassava Crepes)
- Cachorro-Quente Brasileiro (Brazilian Hot Dog)
- Salpicão (Brazilian Chicken Salad)
- Torresmo (Crispy Pork Cracklings)
- Empada de Palmito (Heart of Palm Pastry)
- Vinagrete (Brazilian Salsa)
- Maionese de Batata (Brazilian Potato Salad)
- Mocotó (Cow's Foot Stew)
- Suco de Cupuaçu (Cupuaçu Juice)
- Açaí na Tigela (Açaí Bowl)
- Batida de Coco (Coconut Cocktail)
- Quirera (Corn Grits with Pork)
- Doce de Leite (Brazilian Dulce de Leche)

Feijoada (Black Bean Stew)

A rich and hearty black bean stew with pork and beef, traditionally served with rice and orange slices.

Ingredients:

- 2 cups black beans
- 1 lb pork ribs
- ½ lb smoked sausage, sliced
- ½ lb beef jerky, soaked and chopped
- 1 onion, chopped
- 4 cloves garlic, minced
- 2 bay leaves
- Salt and pepper to taste

Instructions:

1. Soak black beans overnight.
2. Cook beans with bay leaves until tender.
3. Sauté onion and garlic, add meats, and cook.
4. Combine with beans and simmer for 1 hour.
5. Serve with rice, collard greens, and orange slices.

Pão de Queijo (Cheese Bread)

Chewy cheese bread made with tapioca flour.

Ingredients:

- 2 cups tapioca flour
- 1 cup milk
- ½ cup butter
- 1 cup grated Parmesan cheese
- 2 eggs

Instructions:

1. Boil milk and butter, then mix with tapioca flour.
2. Let cool, then add cheese and eggs.
3. Form small balls and bake at 375°F (190°C) for 25 minutes.

Moqueca (Brazilian Fish Stew)

A fragrant fish stew with coconut milk and dendê oil.

Ingredients:

- 1 lb white fish fillets
- 1 onion, sliced
- 1 bell pepper, sliced
- 2 tomatoes, diced
- 1 cup coconut milk
- 2 tbsp dendê (palm) oil
- 2 cloves garlic, minced
- 1 lime (juice)
- Salt and pepper to taste

Instructions:

1. Marinate fish with lime juice and salt.
2. Layer onions, peppers, tomatoes, and fish in a pot.
3. Add coconut milk and simmer for 20 minutes.
4. Stir in dendê oil before serving.

Coxinha (Chicken Croquettes)

Deep-fried, teardrop-shaped chicken croquettes.

Ingredients:

- 2 cups shredded chicken
- 1 onion, chopped
- 2 cups chicken broth
- 2 cups flour
- ½ cup cream cheese
- 2 eggs
- 1 cup breadcrumbs
- Oil for frying

Instructions:

1. Sauté onion, add chicken and cream cheese.
2. Boil broth, stir in flour, and knead into dough.
3. Shape dough around chicken filling.
4. Coat in eggs and breadcrumbs, then fry.

Acarajé (Black-Eyed Pea Fritters)

Deep-fried fritters filled with shrimp and vatapá.

Ingredients:

- 2 cups black-eyed peas, soaked
- 1 onion, chopped
- Salt to taste
- 1 cup dried shrimp
- 1 cup vatapá (see below)
- Dendê oil for frying

Instructions:

1. Blend black-eyed peas and onion.
2. Form into patties and fry in dendê oil.
3. Slice open and fill with shrimp and vatapá.

Vatapá (Seafood and Peanut Stew)

A creamy dish made with shrimp, peanuts, and coconut milk.

Ingredients:

- 1 cup dried shrimp
- ½ cup peanuts, ground
- 1 onion, chopped
- 1 cup coconut milk
- 2 slices bread, soaked in milk
- 2 tbsp dendê oil

Instructions:

1. Blend shrimp, peanuts, onion, and bread.
2. Cook with coconut milk and dendê oil.
3. Simmer until thick.

Escondidinho de Carne Seca (Cassava and Dried Beef Casserole)

A layered casserole with mashed cassava and dried beef.

Ingredients:

- 1 lb dried beef, shredded
- 2 cups mashed cassava
- 1 onion, chopped
- ½ cup milk
- ½ cup cheese, grated

Instructions:

1. Sauté beef with onion.
2. Mix cassava with milk.
3. Layer cassava, beef, and cheese in a dish.
4. Bake at 375°F (190°C) for 20 minutes.

Bobó de Camarão (Shrimp in Cassava Cream)

A creamy shrimp dish with coconut milk and cassava purée.

Ingredients:

- 1 lb shrimp
- 1 onion, chopped
- 1 cup mashed cassava
- 1 cup coconut milk
- 2 tbsp dendê oil
- Salt and pepper

Instructions:

1. Sauté onion, add shrimp and cook.
2. Stir in cassava and coconut milk.
3. Finish with dendê oil.

Farofa (Toasted Cassava Flour)

A crunchy and flavorful side dish made with toasted cassava flour.

Ingredients:

- 2 cups cassava flour
- 2 tbsp butter
- 1 onion, chopped
- ½ cup bacon, chopped
- Salt to taste

Instructions:

1. Sauté onion and bacon in butter.
2. Add cassava flour and toast until golden.

Arroz Carreteiro (Tropeiro's Rice)

A rustic rice dish made with sun-dried beef and vegetables.

Ingredients:

- 2 cups rice
- 1 lb carne de sol (sun-dried beef), chopped
- 1 onion, chopped
- 2 cloves garlic, minced
- 1 tomato, diced
- 1 bell pepper, chopped
- 2 tbsp oil
- 4 cups beef broth
- Salt and pepper to taste

Instructions:

1. Sauté onion, garlic, and beef in oil.
2. Add tomatoes, bell pepper, and rice.
3. Pour in broth and simmer until rice is tender.

Tutu de Feijão (Mashed Beans with Flour)

A hearty bean dish thickened with cassava flour.

Ingredients:

- 2 cups cooked black beans
- ½ cup cassava flour (farinha de mandioca)
- 1 onion, chopped
- 2 cloves garlic, minced
- ½ cup bacon, chopped
- Salt and pepper to taste

Instructions:

1. Sauté bacon, onion, and garlic.
2. Add beans and mash slightly.
3. Stir in cassava flour until thickened.

Carne de Sol (Sun-Dried Beef)

A traditional salted and dried beef dish, served grilled or fried.

Ingredients:

- 2 lbs beef (sirloin or flank)
- ½ cup coarse salt

Instructions:

1. Rub beef with salt and let dry for 24 hours.
2. Rinse excess salt, then grill or pan-fry.

Bolo de Rolo (Rolled Cake)

A thinly rolled sponge cake with layers of guava paste.

Ingredients:

- 2 cups flour
- 1 cup sugar
- 4 eggs
- ½ cup butter
- 1 tsp vanilla extract
- 1 cup guava paste, melted

Instructions:

1. Beat butter, sugar, and eggs until fluffy.
2. Add flour and vanilla.
3. Bake thin layers, spread guava paste, and roll tightly.

Brigadeiro (Chocolate Fudge Balls)

Classic Brazilian chocolate truffles rolled in sprinkles.

Ingredients:

- 1 can sweetened condensed milk
- 2 tbsp cocoa powder
- 1 tbsp butter
- Chocolate sprinkles

Instructions:

1. Cook condensed milk, cocoa, and butter until thickened.
2. Cool, roll into balls, and coat in sprinkles.

Quindim (Coconut Egg Custard)

A bright yellow coconut custard with a glossy top.

Ingredients:

- 6 egg yolks
- 1 cup sugar
- 1 cup shredded coconut
- 2 tbsp butter

Instructions:

1. Mix all ingredients and pour into greased molds.
2. Bake in a water bath at 350°F (175°C) for 40 minutes.

Beijinho (Coconut Truffle)

A coconut version of brigadeiro, rolled in coconut flakes.

Ingredients:

- 1 can sweetened condensed milk
- 1 tbsp butter
- 1 cup shredded coconut
- Granulated sugar for coating

Instructions:

1. Cook condensed milk, butter, and coconut until thick.
2. Cool, roll into balls, and coat in sugar.

Manjar Branco (Coconut Pudding)

A creamy coconut pudding topped with caramelized prunes.

Ingredients:

- 2 cups coconut milk
- ½ cup cornstarch
- ½ cup sugar
- 1 cup prunes
- ½ cup sugar (for syrup)

Instructions:

1. Cook coconut milk, cornstarch, and sugar until thickened.
2. Pour into a mold and let set.
3. Simmer prunes with sugar for syrup.

Pudim de Leite (Brazilian Flan)

A smooth caramel flan made with condensed milk.

Ingredients:

- 1 can sweetened condensed milk
- 1 can whole milk
- 3 eggs
- ½ cup sugar (for caramel)

Instructions:

1. Melt sugar into caramel and coat a mold.
2. Blend condensed milk, milk, and eggs.
3. Bake in a water bath at 350°F (175°C) for 1 hour.

Canjica (Sweet Corn Pudding)

A comforting dessert made with white corn and coconut milk.

Ingredients:

- 2 cups white corn (hominy), soaked overnight
- 4 cups milk
- 1 cup coconut milk
- ½ cup sugar
- 1 cinnamon stick

Instructions:

1. Cook corn in milk until soft.
2. Add coconut milk, sugar, and cinnamon.
3. Simmer until thickened.

Curau de Milho (Sweet Corn Custard)

A creamy and sweet corn-based dessert with a smooth texture.

Ingredients:

- 4 ears fresh corn (or 2 cups corn kernels)
- 2 cups whole milk
- ½ cup sugar
- 1 tsp butter
- Cinnamon powder for garnish

Instructions:

1. Blend corn with milk and strain.
2. Heat mixture with sugar and butter until thickened.
3. Pour into bowls, cool, and sprinkle with cinnamon.

Cuscuz Paulista (Savory Cornmeal Cake)

A firm, flavorful cornmeal dish packed with vegetables and seafood.

Ingredients:

- 2 cups cornmeal
- 3 cups broth
- ½ cup tomato sauce
- 1 onion, chopped
- 2 cloves garlic, minced
- 1 cup shrimp or sardines
- ½ cup green peas
- ½ cup black olives
- 1 boiled egg, sliced

Instructions:

1. Sauté onion, garlic, and seafood.
2. Add broth and tomato sauce, then stir in cornmeal.
3. Pour into a mold, press, and cool before slicing.

Empadão (Brazilian Pot Pie)

A flaky pastry filled with a creamy, savory filling.

Ingredients:

- 2 cups flour
- ½ cup butter
- 1 egg
- ½ cup milk
- 1 tsp salt
- 2 cups shredded chicken
- 1 cup cream cheese
- ½ cup olives

Instructions:

1. Mix flour, butter, egg, and milk to form dough.
2. Line a pie dish with dough, fill with chicken mixture, and cover with dough.
3. Bake at 375°F (190°C) until golden.

Pastel (Fried Pastry with Filling)

A crispy fried pastry stuffed with cheese, meat, or heart of palm.

Ingredients:

- 2 cups flour
- ½ cup warm water
- 1 tbsp oil
- ½ tsp salt
- Filling of choice (cheese, beef, chicken)

Instructions:

1. Mix dough ingredients, roll thin, and cut into circles.
2. Fill, seal edges, and fry until golden.

Bolinho de Bacalhau (Salt Cod Fritters)

Crispy fritters made from salt cod and mashed potatoes.

Ingredients:

- 1 cup salt cod, soaked and shredded
- 2 potatoes, boiled and mashed
- 1 egg
- 2 tbsp flour
- 1 tbsp parsley, chopped
- Oil for frying

Instructions:

1. Mix all ingredients into a dough.
2. Shape into balls and deep fry until golden.

Caldo Verde (Green Soup)

A hearty soup with kale, potatoes, and sausage.

Ingredients:

- 3 potatoes, peeled and diced
- 4 cups chicken broth
- 1 chorizo sausage, sliced
- 2 cups kale, chopped
- 1 onion, chopped

Instructions:

1. Cook potatoes and onion in broth, then blend.
2. Add sausage and kale, simmer for 5 minutes.

Sopa de Mandioquinha (Parsnip Soup)

A smooth and creamy soup made with Brazilian parsnip.

Ingredients:

- 3 parsnips, peeled and diced
- 4 cups broth
- 1 onion, chopped
- 1 tbsp butter
- Salt and pepper

Instructions:

1. Sauté onion in butter, add parsnips and broth.
2. Simmer, blend until smooth, and season.

Baião de Dois (Rice and Beans with Cheese)

A traditional Brazilian dish with a mix of rice, beans, and cheese.

Ingredients:

- 1 cup rice
- 1 cup black-eyed peas, cooked
- ½ cup queijo coalho (or firm cheese)
- 1 onion, chopped
- 2 cloves garlic, minced
- 1 tbsp butter

Instructions:

1. Sauté onion and garlic, add rice and beans.
2. Stir in cheese and butter before serving.

Churrasco (Brazilian BBQ)

A classic Brazilian barbecue with different cuts of meat.

Ingredients:

- 2 lbs beef, pork, or chicken
- 1 tbsp salt
- 1 tbsp olive oil

Instructions:

1. Rub meat with salt and oil.
2. Grill over open flame until charred.

Picanha (Grilled Top Sirloin)

Brazil's most famous grilled steak, seasoned simply with salt.

Ingredients:

- 2 lbs picanha (top sirloin cap)
- 1 tbsp coarse salt

Instructions:

1. Cut into thick slices, season with salt.
2. Grill to desired doneness.

Frango com Quiabo (Chicken with Okra)

A rich, stewed chicken dish with fresh okra.

Ingredients:

- 2 lbs chicken, cut into pieces
- 2 cups okra, sliced
- 1 onion, chopped
- 2 cloves garlic, minced
- 2 cups chicken broth

Instructions:

1. Sauté onion, garlic, and chicken.
2. Add okra and broth, simmer until tender.

Moela de Frango (Chicken Gizzards)

A hearty and flavorful gizzard stew, popular in Brazilian cuisine.

Ingredients:

- 1 lb chicken gizzards, cleaned
- 1 onion, chopped
- 2 cloves garlic, minced
- 2 tomatoes, chopped
- ½ cup bell peppers, chopped
- 1 cup chicken broth
- 1 tbsp olive oil
- Salt and pepper to taste

Instructions:

1. Heat oil in a pan, sauté onion and garlic.
2. Add gizzards and cook until browned.
3. Stir in tomatoes, peppers, and broth.
4. Simmer for 30–40 minutes until tender.

Dobradinha (Tripe Stew)

A slow-cooked dish made with tripe, beans, and sausage.

Ingredients:

- 1 lb beef tripe, cleaned and cut
- 1 cup white beans, cooked
- 1 sausage, sliced
- 1 onion, chopped
- 2 cloves garlic, minced
- 1 tomato, chopped
- 4 cups beef broth

Instructions:

1. Boil tripe for 30 minutes, drain, and set aside.
2. Sauté onion, garlic, and sausage.
3. Add tripe, beans, tomato, and broth.
4. Simmer for 1 hour until tender.

Arroz com Pequi (Rice with Pequi Fruit)

A regional dish from Goiás, featuring the unique pequi fruit.

Ingredients:

- 2 cups rice
- 4 pequi fruits, halved
- 1 onion, chopped
- 2 cloves garlic, minced
- 4 cups chicken broth
- 1 tbsp olive oil
- Salt to taste

Instructions:

1. Sauté onion and garlic in oil.
2. Add pequi and rice, stirring well.
3. Pour in broth, cover, and cook until rice is tender.

Carne Louca (Shredded Beef Stew)

A flavorful shredded beef dish served in sandwiches or with rice.

Ingredients:

- 2 lbs beef (chuck roast or flank steak)
- 1 onion, sliced
- 2 cloves garlic, minced
- 1 bell pepper, sliced
- 1 tomato, chopped
- 1 cup beef broth
- 1 tbsp olive oil
- Salt and pepper

Instructions:

1. Sear beef in oil, then add onion and garlic.
2. Add broth and simmer for 2 hours.
3. Shred beef and mix with sautéed peppers and tomatoes.

Feijão Tropeiro (Pinto Beans with Sausage)

A hearty bean dish with cassava flour and sausage.

Ingredients:

- 2 cups cooked pinto beans
- 1 sausage, sliced
- ½ cup bacon, diced
- 1 onion, chopped
- 2 cloves garlic, minced
- ½ cup cassava flour
- Salt and pepper

Instructions:

1. Fry bacon and sausage until crispy.
2. Add onion, garlic, and beans.
3. Stir in cassava flour and mix well.

Galinhada (Chicken and Rice)

A one-pot chicken and rice dish from Minas Gerais.

Ingredients:

- 1 lb chicken pieces
- 2 cups rice
- 1 onion, chopped
- 2 cloves garlic, minced
- 1 tomato, chopped
- 4 cups chicken broth
- 1 tsp turmeric
- Salt and pepper

Instructions:

1. Sauté onion and garlic, then brown chicken.
2. Add rice, tomato, turmeric, and broth.
3. Cover and cook until rice is done.

Espetinho de Coração (Grilled Chicken Hearts)

A popular Brazilian street food snack.

Ingredients:

- 1 lb chicken hearts
- 2 tbsp olive oil
- 2 cloves garlic, minced
- 1 tbsp vinegar
- Salt and pepper

Instructions:

1. Marinate hearts in oil, garlic, vinegar, salt, and pepper.
2. Skewer and grill until browned.

Tapioca (Cassava Crepes)

A simple and gluten-free Brazilian snack or breakfast.

Ingredients:

- 1 cup tapioca flour
- Water (to moisten flour)
- Fillings (cheese, condensed milk, ham)

Instructions:

1. Sprinkle moist tapioca flour into a hot pan.
2. Cook for 2 minutes, then add filling.
3. Fold and serve warm.

Cachorro-Quente Brasileiro (Brazilian Hot Dog)

A loaded hot dog with a variety of toppings.

Ingredients:

- 4 hot dog buns
- 4 sausages
- 1 onion, chopped
- 1 tomato, chopped
- ½ cup corn
- ½ cup mashed potatoes
- ¼ cup grated cheese
- Potato sticks for topping

Instructions:

1. Sauté onion and tomato, then add sausages.
2. Assemble hot dog with toppings.

Salpicão (Brazilian Chicken Salad)

A creamy, crunchy chicken salad with apples and raisins.

Ingredients:

- 2 cups shredded chicken
- ½ cup mayonnaise
- ½ cup carrots, grated
- ½ cup apples, diced
- ¼ cup raisins
- ¼ cup green olives, sliced

Instructions:

1. Mix all ingredients in a bowl.
2. Chill before serving.

Torresmo (Crispy Pork Cracklings)

A crunchy and flavorful fried pork belly snack.

Ingredients:

- 1 lb pork belly, cut into small cubes
- 1 tbsp salt
- 1 tsp baking soda (for extra crispiness)
- 2 cups oil (for frying)

Instructions:

1. Season pork belly with salt and baking soda. Let sit for 30 minutes.
2. Heat oil in a deep pan and fry pork over medium heat until golden and crispy.
3. Remove and drain on paper towels before serving.

Empada de Palmito (Heart of Palm Pastry)

A savory, buttery pastry filled with a creamy heart of palm mixture.

Ingredients:

- **Dough:**
    - 2 cups flour
    - ½ cup butter
    - 1 egg
    - ½ tsp salt
    - ¼ cup cold water
- **Filling:**
    - 1 cup chopped heart of palm
    - ½ cup milk
    - 1 tbsp butter
    - 1 tbsp flour
    - Salt and pepper

Instructions:

1. Mix dough ingredients and refrigerate for 30 minutes.
2. For the filling, cook butter and flour, then add milk and heart of palm. Cook until thickened.
3. Roll out dough, fill with mixture, cover with another layer of dough, and bake at 350°F (180°C) for 25 minutes.

Vinagrete (Brazilian Salsa)

A fresh and tangy tomato-based condiment served with meats and churrasco.

Ingredients:

- 2 tomatoes, diced
- 1 onion, finely chopped
- ½ bell pepper, diced
- 2 tbsp vinegar
- 3 tbsp olive oil
- Salt and pepper
- 2 tbsp chopped parsley

Instructions:

1. Mix all ingredients in a bowl.
2. Let sit for 10 minutes before serving.

Maionese de Batata (Brazilian Potato Salad)

A creamy potato salad, often served at barbecues.

Ingredients:

- 3 potatoes, diced and boiled
- 1 carrot, diced and boiled
- ½ cup peas
- ½ cup mayonnaise
- 1 tbsp mustard
- 1 boiled egg, chopped
- Salt and pepper

Instructions:

1. Mix all ingredients in a bowl.
2. Refrigerate before serving.

Mocotó (Cow's Foot Stew)

A rich and gelatinous stew made with cow's feet and beans.

Ingredients:

- 2 lbs cow's feet, cleaned and chopped
- 1 onion, chopped
- 2 cloves garlic, minced
- 1 tomato, chopped
- 1 cup white beans, cooked
- 4 cups beef broth
- 1 tbsp olive oil

Instructions:

1. Sauté onion and garlic in oil.
2. Add cow's feet, tomato, and broth. Simmer for 2 hours.
3. Add cooked beans and serve warm.

Suco de Cupuaçu (Cupuaçu Juice)

A refreshing tropical fruit juice from the Amazon.

Ingredients:

- 1 cup cupuaçu pulp
- 2 cups cold water
- 2 tbsp sugar
- Ice cubes

Instructions:

1. Blend all ingredients until smooth.
2. Serve over ice.

Açaí na Tigela (Açaí Bowl)

A thick and nutritious açaí smoothie bowl with toppings.

Ingredients:

- 1 cup frozen açaí pulp
- 1 banana
- ½ cup apple juice
- Granola, sliced bananas, and honey for topping

Instructions:

1. Blend açaí, banana, and juice until thick.
2. Pour into a bowl and top with granola, banana, and honey.

Batida de Coco (Coconut Cocktail)

A sweet and creamy Brazilian coconut cocktail.

Ingredients:

- 1 cup coconut milk
- ½ cup condensed milk
- ½ cup cachaça (or vodka)
- Ice cubes

Instructions:

1. Blend all ingredients with ice until smooth.
2. Serve chilled.

Quirera (Corn Grits with Pork)

A rustic and hearty dish made with corn grits and pork.

Ingredients:

- 1 cup corn grits
- ½ lb pork ribs or sausage
- 1 onion, chopped
- 2 cloves garlic, minced
- 4 cups chicken broth
- Salt and pepper

Instructions:

1. Sauté onion and garlic, then add pork.
2. Stir in grits and broth. Simmer until thick and soft.

Doce de Leite (Brazilian Dulce de Leche)

A creamy caramelized milk spread or dessert.

Ingredients:

- 4 cups whole milk
- 1 ½ cups sugar
- ½ tsp baking soda

Instructions:

1. Simmer milk, sugar, and baking soda over low heat.
2. Stir continuously for about 1 hour until thick and golden.
3. Let cool before serving.

www.ingramcontent.com/pod-product-compliance
Lightning Source LLC
LaVergne TN
LVHW081332060526
838201LV00055B/2587